MW01251477

He Is
RISEN!

He Is RISEN!

The Easter Women
Jesus Returns to Heaven
The Coming of the Holy Spirit

An ARCH BOOKS Gift Collection

*An Inspirational Press Book
for Children*

First Inspirational Press edition published in 1999.

Inspirational Press
A division of BBS Publishing Corporation
386 Park Avenue South
New York, NY 10016

Inspirational Press is a registered trademark of BBS Publishing Corporation.

Published by arrangement with Concordia Publishing House,
3558 S. Jefferson Ave., St. Louis, MO 63118-3968.

Library of Congress Catalog Card Number: 98-75451

ISBN: 0-88486-229-1

Printed in Mexico

The
Easter Women

The Easter Women
Luke 7:36–8:3; 23:55–24:12; John 20:1–
18 for children

Written by Carol Greene
Illustrated by
Betty Wind

As Jesus went traveling from village to town,
Teaching and showing God's ways,
Some men (there were twelve)
    walked along with the Lord;
They helped, and they learned and gave praise.

But not only men followed Jesus on earth;
Women believed in Him, too.
Some helped from their homes,
　　and some traveled along,
Doing everything that they could do.

There was Mary, His mother; Salome another;
And Mary the mother of James,
Joanna, Susanna, and quite a few more
Who helped (but we don't know their names).

Mary of Magdala followed Him, too,
Though once she had been very bad.
From seven demons her Lord set her free;
So He was the best Friend she had.

Once at a party, she fell on her knees
And washed Jesus' feet with her tears.
She dried with her hair, anointed them too.
The host watched with self-righteous sneers.

"This woman is wicked," he said to himself,
"And Jesus cannot even see."
But Jesus *could* see—inside the man's mind.
"Now, Simon, you listen to Me.

"When I arrived, you did nothing for Me,
No water, no oil, and no touch.
But *this* woman loves Me with all of her heart.
You see, I've forgiven her much.

So Mary of Magdala
    knew the Lord's peace;
It sang in her heart
    like a song.
When the Lord said, "Let's go
    to Jerusalem now."
She packed up
    and went right along.

But there in the city, whispers grew loud.
Such terrible things people said!
When Mary heard them, her peace flew away.
The song in her heart turned to dread.

"Could they kill Jesus?" she wondered aloud.
"Can such ugly rumors be true?"
No one could answer, no one could say,
Because they were wondering too.

A Friday it was when she and her friends
Watched as a cross split the sky.
On it hung Jesus, the true Son of God.
They watched—and they saw Jesus die.

How empty they felt as they stumbled away
And went to fix spices . . . and cry.
"I now will anoint Him again," Mary thought,
"But this time—oh, why did He die?"

They went with their spices out to the tomb
On Sunday, just before dawn.
"The stone is rolled back! No one is here!"
The body of Jesus was gone.

To Peter and John,
    who were Jesus' good friends,
They ran with their hearts beating hard.
"Someone took Jesus! His body is gone!
Oh, what have they done with our Lord?"

Off to the tomb hurried Peter and John.
Mary came panting behind.
The men went on in . . . but she stood alone,
Wondering what they would find.

They found the new linens
    they'd used for His wrap,
But forgot what the Scriptures had said.
His body was gone, but they didn't believe
That Jesus was no longer dead!

Off ran the men, leaving Mary to cry . . .
But finally she peeked in the tomb.
Two angels were there, dressed all in white.
How awesome they shone in that room!

"Why are you crying?" asked a kind voice.
"Whom are you looking for here?"
A man stood behind her—
        the gardener perhaps?—
Poor Mary; her eyes were not clear.

"Mary!" He called her. And then Mary knew.
"Rabonni! My teacher!" she said.
"Don't touch me," He said;
   "tell the others I live!"
So back through the streets Mary fled.

The song in her heart soared up like a bird.
She heard it again and again.
"Jesus the Savior has trampled down death.
He lives! Alleluia! Amen!"

DEAR PARENTS:

Of all of Jesus' disciples, Mary Magdalene was the first to see the risen Lord (Mark 16:9). Mary responded in awe and joy and then in obedience and witness: she "went and said to the disciples, 'I have seen the Lord' " (John 20:18 RSV).

Mary, most likely from the town of Magdala on the southwest shore of the Sea of Galilee, from which she derives her name, joined Jesus' immediate family of followers near the beginning of His Galilean ministry. Like Joanna and Susanna, Mary helped support Jesus and His disciples and "provided for them out of [her] own means" (Luke 8:3).

Luke also tells us that Jesus cast out of Mary "seven demons"; she responded to her Master's love, not only with her "means, " but also with a bold witness and a life of faith. Along with the apostle John and some of the other women who followed Jesus, she did not desert her Savior at His crucifixion: "Standing by the cross of Jesus were His mother, and His mother's sister, Mary the wife of Clopas, and Mary Magdalene" (John 19:25). Brave Peter and most of Jesus' beloved followers were nowhere in sight.

Share with your child the joy of Mary's Easter discovery, for Mary's Savior—and ours—has arisen indeed and has won each of us "from all sins, from death, and from the power of the devil."

The song in her heart soared up like a bird.
She heard it again and again.
"Jesus the Savior has trampled down death.
He lives! Alleluia! Amen!"

THE EDITOR

JESUS
RETURNS
~TO~
HEAVEN

Matthew 28:11–20
Luke 24:36–53
Acts 1:1–12 for Children

Written by Robert Baden
Illustrated by Michael Hackett

Jesus rose on Easter Day
Alive, no longer dead;
Though many heard the news with joy,
Some doubted what was said.

"Did Jesus really die?" they asked;
"Did Jesus really rise?"
And those who wanted Jesus dead
Created evil lies.

"No, Jesus didn't really rise,"
These evil people said;
"His body was removed at night,
But Jesus is still dead."

So everyone would know the truth,
Our Lord took forty days
To show He was indeed alive
In many different ways:

He walked, He talked, He ate, He showed
His wounded hands and side;
And soon the truth of Easter Day
Had traveled far and wide.

Then Jesus said, "All power on earth
And heaven belongs to Me;
Soon I'll send special power to you
So all of you can be

"My messengers throughout the world;
Here's what I hope you'll do:
Go share with everyone the love
That I have shared with you.

"First tell those in Jerusalem,
Then all in every land,
That I have lived and died for them;
Make sure they understand.

"Make them disciples, teach them how
To live; and when that's done
Baptize them in the name of God—
Father, Spirit, Son."

Then Jesus smiled and said, "My friends,
This promise now I give:
I'll be with you each hour and day
As long as you will live.

"Wait until the Spirit comes
To give My power to you;
Once He has come—it won't be long—
You'll know just what to do."

Then Jesus led His faithful friends
To a hill outside of town.
And there He smiled and hugged each one
And asked them to sit down.

He blessed them all, raised up His hands,
And before their very eyes,
Began to lift up off the ground
And rise into the skies!

His friends jumped quickly to their feet
And shouted loud and long!
They kept on watching till their Lord
Was hidden by a cloud.

"I can't believe it!" one man said,
Gazing toward the sky.
"What does this mean?" another cried,
"Why did He leave us? Why?"

All kept on looking at the spot
Where Jesus disappeared,
When suddenly they sensed that someone
Else had just appeared.

There standing by them were two men,
Both dressed in shining white;
"Why are you looking up?" one asked;
"Everything's all right.

"Yes, Jesus now has left the earth,
But He'll come again one day;
And then He'll take all who believe
To heaven with Him to stay."

This message filled their hearts with joy;
How glad they were to hear it!
They worshiped God and went to wait
For the coming Holy Spirit.

Dear Parents:

Help your child find Ascension Day—40 days after Easter—on a calendar. Circle the date and plan a special celebration for that day. As you plan, discuss the Great Commission—Jesus' command to His disciples and to us to proclaim His Gospel in our own community and throughout the world.

Roleplay witnessing your faith with your child. Then decide on someone in your neighborhood with whom you can share God's love. Give that person a homemade gift or card, expressing Jesus' care and sharing your faith in Him.

If your church uses offering envelopes, show one to your child. Explain that part of the money you give in the offering helps missionaries proclaim the good news that Jesus died and rose again for all people. Decide on a way your child can earn money to support world mission work.

Pray with your child and thank Jesus for getting your rooms ready in heaven. Ask the blessing of His Holy Spirit as you share your faith with your child, your neighbors, and people throughout the world.

The Editor

The Coming of the Holy Spirit

Acts 2:1–41 for children
Written by Robert Baden
Illustrated by Reg Sandland

When Jesus left the grave alive
  That first great Easter Day,
He told the friends that loved Him so
  That soon He'd go away.

"Then *you,* my friends, must tell the world
  My story—all must hear it.
To give you power to do this job,
  I'm sending you God's Spirit."

Then Jesus went back home to heaven,
    And His friends felt sad and lost.
But He sent the Spirit like He said
    On the day called Pentecost.

That morning in the room where
    Jesus' friends spent time in prayer,
A sudden noise like rushing wind
    Roared in as they met there.

And when the sound at last calmed down,
   On every person's head
A tiny flame of fire stood,
   Bright and warm and red.

"Just what is going on?" one asked;
    "Is this what Jesus sent?"
"What's happening here?" "I'm scared!" "Me too!"
    They wondered what it meant.

Then gradually inside of them
    A strange new feeling grew.
It started in their hearts, and then
    It filled their bodies too.

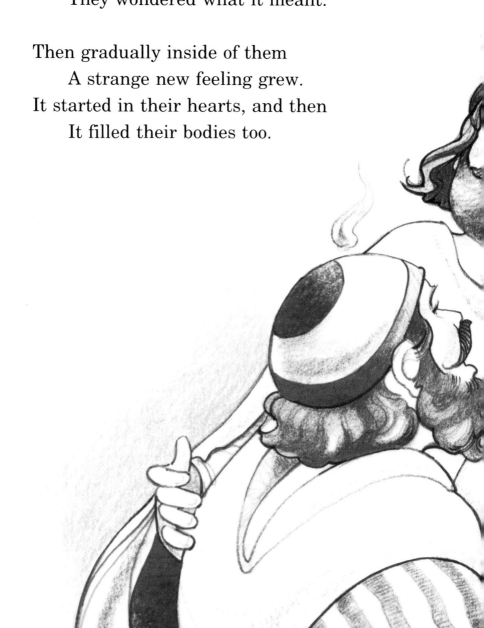

This was the gift that Jesus sent;
    It gave them power to speak
Languages like African,
    Arabian, and Greek.

They ran outside to share the news
    With folks from every land.
It made no difference where they lived;
    Each one could understand.

"How can they speak like this?" one said.
    "It's a miracle, I think!"
Most were amazed, but others said,
    "They've had too much to drink!"

Then Peter, chief disciple, stood
    And told the growing crowd,
"The men you see aren't drunk but filled
    With special power from God!

"He's given us the power to speak
    So all can understand
This story that we want to tell
    To those from every land:

"Our Savior, Jesus, Son of God,
Came down to live on earth.
He came to Bethlehem, and angels
Sang about His birth.

"When Jesus grew, He told why God
　　Had sent Him from above.
He healed the sick, He fed the poor,
　　He lived His life in love.

"And then you killed this Son of God;
  You nailed Him to a cross.
You buried Him in a grave of stone,
  Not knowing what you'd lost.

"But three days later He arose—
    Alive, no longer dead!
His death has washed away your sins;
    Come, follow Him instead!"

The people heard what Peter said
    And asked him what to do.
"Turn from your sins and be baptized
    God's calling each of you!"

That day, three thousand people joined
  The church at Peter's call.
And that same Jesus still today
  Is calling to us all.

He's also given each of us
  New power from the Spirit.
Let's share His story everywhere
  So all the world can hear it!

Dear Parents:

You may wish to plan a birthday party with your child as you read this book, for as these events took place, Pentecost became the birthday of the Christian church. Devout Jews from all over the world were gathered in Jerusalem to celebrate Pentecost, a harvest festival held the 50th day after the Sabbath following Passover. Three thousand people, upon hearing Christ's Gospel proclaimed in their own language, repented of their sins and were baptized.

The power of His Holy Spirit transformed not only the disciples' tongues, but their entire lives. These formerly timid men boldly proclaimed the saving work of Jesus so that all who heard them were stirred by the power of the Gospel.

Jesus has given you and your child the same job He gave His first disciples, the task of proclaiming His Good News of salvation to all nations (Matt. 28:19–20). The Holy Spirit has worked in you and your child saving faith and gives you the power you need to share God's Word. Celebrate the birthday of the Christian church. Pray that you may boldly share the Good News about Jesus with those around you.

The Editor